000 INDEPENDENT LEGIONS PUBLISHING

SPECIALTY PRESS AWARD RECIPIENT

ARTIFACTS
BY BRUCE BOSTON

ISBN: 978-88-31959-06-3
COPYRIGHT (EDITION) ©2018 INDEPENDENT LEGIONS PUBLISHING
COPYRIGHT (WORK) 2018©BRUCE BOSTON
COVER ART BY WENDY SABER CORE

ALL RIGHTS RESERVED
JULY 2018

ARTIFACTS
Bruce Boston

Poems in this collection have appeared or are forthcoming, in the following periodicals and anthologies: *Analog, Aoife's Kiss, Asimov's SF Magazine, Bête Noire, Chiral Mad 3, Daily Science Fiction, Devilfish Review, Dreams and Nightmares, Grievous Angel, Illumen, Into Darkness Peering, New Myths, Polu Texni, The HWA Poetry Showcase, Illumen, In Space No One Can Hear You Scream, Tales from the Lake, The Audient Void, The 2018 Rhysling Anthology, The Journal of Compressed Creative Arts, The Literary Hatchet, Silver Blade, Star*Line, Tales of the Talisman.*

The following poems appear here for the first time: "Discovering the Miraculous, Engines of the Future, Final Passage, Intuitive Leap, Malign and Chronic Recreation, Nineteenth Century Rebellion, Pan's Descent, Savage Civilization, Surreal Lust, With Blood So Dark".

Contents

- 11 Unwritten
- 12 A Grand Guignol Kind of Night
- 14 A Dangerous Reading
- 16 Blurred Future
- 16 Vampire Fortuneteller
- 16 A Dubious Talent
- 17 Forever Tracking
- 20 Exiled to Hastur
- 24 She Walks in Yellow to Please Her Lord
- 26 Beheading the King
- 29 Royal Visitation
- 30 The Hallucinogenic Gourmand
- 32 Triptych of the Tower
- 34 Heroes of Indefinite Beauty
- 35 The Dream Thief
- 37 Mortal Remains
- 38 First to Draw
- 39 Nineteenth Century Rebellion
- 40 Savage Civilization
- 41 Memories of the Dead
- 42 Revenants
- 43 Final Passage
- 44 Sailors Evermore
- 48 The Music of Angels
- 50 Salamanders: Fire
- 51 Gnomes: Earth
- 53 Pan's Descent
- 55 One More Shade in the Shadow City
- 57 Beware the Night Creatures

58	Full Moon Forecast
58	Blood Bite
59	The Last Gypsies
60	Disclosing the Miraculous
61	Synesthesia
62	When Words Take Flight
64	With Blood So Dark
67	Cambrian Flashback
68	Beyond Symmetry
70	Reflecting on Reflections
70	Inconclusive View
71	Mirror Madness
72	Enough
74	Intuitive Leaps
75	Wife of a Particle Physicist
76	Birth of an Astrophysicist
76	Paint It Black
77	Engines of the Future
78	Failing Masterpiece
79	Space Junk
80	CyberDebris
81	Malign and Chronic Recreation
82	Maximus 3000
84	Surreal Bucket List #3
85	Surreal Axioms
86	Surreal Lust
86	The Surreal Monster
87	The Surreal Fountain Pen

artifact

an object made
by a human being, typically
an item of cultural or historical interest

Unwritten

The only real history
of the human species
lies in the vanished
memories of the dead.

A Grand Guignol Kind of Night

The right kind of night for
a theatre of the dark absurd,
an enchanted evening's folly
for addict-connoisseurs
of murder most foul.

Shadows were gathering,
in the salon, the greenhouse,
the library of countless shelves,
dread passions soon released
 in the night, voices raised
in anger, three screams,
the barking of a dog.

Morning would find
blood in the back garden,
a scimitar discarded
on the study floor,
the stoked remains
of belladonna dreams
in the sunlit haze
of unaired rooms.

On the screened porch
the chairs and tables
tossed this way and that,
broken glass and the
residue of spilt drinks

scattered across the tiles.

Bodies would be
trucked to the morgue
in the county meat wagon,
thick with the scents
of death and horror.

By noon of the next day
the slaughter and wreckage
will have streamed away,
furniture properly placed,
dead bodies resurrected,
shifting shadows restored,
prepared for one more
dark enchanted evening
for addict-connoisseurs
of murder most foul.

A Dangerous Reading

Being a lady of diverse preoccupations,
primarily preternatural, Madame Tarot
turns her head from the street and
tells me that anything is possible.
We pass the pipe from hand to hand.
The rain rallies against the window,
softly blurring hillsides and trees.

"Darjeeling or jasmine?" she asks,
pouring from a single pot inlaid
with gold symbols on black slate.
Perhaps I have visited here more
than once too often, watching the
cards shift in the yellow lamplight.

Down the stairs shambles her pet
and familiar. Today its shaggy
coat of chameleon fur is the
pale rust of old blood stains.
It shakes itself and curls up
on the rug before the fire.

Not for the first time I wonder
what species and sex this creature
could be, but I'll not be the one
to investigate. It outweighs me
by at least twenty pounds and
I have seen rows of razor teeth
glistening in its mercurial coat.

Madame Tarot moves about the room,
drawing shades against the daylight,
switching on a lamp with a fringed
shade to counter the sudden dimness.
She lights the pomegranate incense,
Her hands unfold the velvet cloth.
At moments like this I am sure
she is The Hierophant, Reversed.

She shuffles and riffles the deck.
A blast of wind shakes the window
in its frame and the old house groans.
Her pet stretches and yawns and gives
me a hostile glance. Its coat darkens.

I raise the cup to my lips carefully
and watch the cards begin to turn.

Blurred Future

His fortuneteller
had a cataract
on her third eye.

Vampire Fortuneteller

She reads the veins
in your throat
and only charges
a few drops.

A Dubious Talent

She was a clairvoyant
who could only
foresee the future
of alternate realities.

Forever Tracking
for t. winter-damon

Forever interpreting
ancient texts
as their tattered
scrolls unrolled
within his mind,
treading the borders
of the Axis Mundi
with no more than
an empty leather satchel,
ranging the streets
of Xanadu and Carcosa,
Asgard and Babylon,
tracking like a beast
with a ravenous beast
astride its back,
whispering sacral curses
and foul blessings
to the eldritch winds.

Immersed in dreamtides
and chimerical visions
and cimmerian prophets
whose shadows rose
from the dust of ages,
worshipping priestesses
created for the day,
following transient avatars
down to a dim beach

and the dark sea
of a false dawn
to hear the damp cries
of beached mariners
echoing in his brain.

Intoxicated by secret keys
and magical rings,
obsessed by puzzle boxes
with hidden compartments
only to be opened
by the wisest of men
and most cunning women,
drunk on myth and
history and a tomorrow
that foreshadowed
more than night.

Enthralled by the occult
and the fantastic,
Crowley and Blavatsky,
Faustus and Paracelsus,
poring over maps
revealing the locations
of imagined kingdoms,
Mu and El Dorado,
Atlantis and Shangra-La,
the Archipelago of Dreams,
maps fashioned by madmen
on a transcendental high
over a fifth of Ravens Rum

and a pinch of fly agaric.

Anticipating the excavation
of underwater ruins
and red temples
crumbling to red sand
in some distant desert,
astounded by age-old
architectural mysteries,
the Great Pyramids,
the dour monoliths
of Easter Island,
the astronomical
savvy of Stonehenge.

Awaiting the lab tests
on the Shroud of Turin
and the release of
a revised annotation
of the *Bardol Thodol*,
praying for the miraculous
to snuff the everyday.

Last heard from
traveling to parts unknown,
head down and eyes afire,
carrying no more than
a worn leather satchel
stuffed with worlds.

Exiled to Hastur
after Robert W. Chambers King-in-Yellow stories

Exiled to Hastur,
one of the many dark stars
that rise and fall
in the night sky of Carcosa,
exiled to Hastur
by a Royal Proclamation of the King,
I wander a darkling plain in forever dusk,
its monotony relieved only by
the fetid swamps and tall spectral trees
with their golden apples.

The doctors say I am delusional.
There is no such place as Hastur.
The doctors insist I live in an unreal world,
that I am a patient in a mental hospital
in Washington, D. C.

Yet I know the signature of His Highness
and I have seen the Proclamation
of My Exile and I cannot deny
the evidence of my senses.

*

The golden apples fall to the ground
already rotten, their fruit a sour pulp
sometimes infested by maggots,
yet I eat them nonetheless

for there is nothing else to eat.
I drink the foul water of the swamps
for there is nothing else to drink.

I try to climb the slippery bark
of the spectral black trees
to reach the apples before they rot,
yet the branches prove too fragile.
They will not bear my weight and
I fall and bruise my arm and shoulder.

The doctors claim that I have
injured myself on purpose,
that there are neither trees nor apples,
that there are no fetid swamps,
no darkling plain on which I wander.

Yet I have seen the Yellow Sign,
I understand its full intent,
and the sour taste of the apples
and the wretched swamp water
still cling to my tongue and palate.

*

Sometimes I notice others
walking in the far distance,
accursed exiles like myself,
wandering aimlessly as I do,
yet our paths never cross.

So I travel the dim and
silent landscape of Hastur,
a dusk sky lowering upon me,
condemned to a life of solitude,
ranting aloud about worlds
and loves that I have lost
merely to break the silence,
worlds and loves that become
less and less real even
as I speak their names.

The doctors certify that I am mad
and will keep me here until cured.
The doctors insist that I am delusional,
their changing faces a parade of ignorance.

For I have not forgotten
the pallid corpse trailing
me through the crowds,
nor the way he raised his arm,
pointing the decaying forefinger
of his grossly misshapen hand
in no direction but mine.

*

When I see the shining globe
of Carcosa, golden and majestic
and overwhelming in brilliance
as it glides across the matte
gray of this ever-darkling sky,

I pray to the King in Yellow
to be pardoned and repatriated,
to be forgiven for whatever
transgression I have committed
to offend his Royal Highness.
Or sometimes I pray merely
for the release of a swift death.

The doctors insist I am delusional,
The doctors are only dreams
I create in moments of sanity.

For I have read the Second Act
with its terrifying revelations
and I know the truth.

For I have walked with Camilla
by the scalded sea.

She Walks in Yellow to Please Her Lord
after Robert W. Chambers' King-in-Yellow stories

She who serves her Lord
more than any rank courtesan
in His bloodstained seraglio.
She who severs the swollen
filaments of His deranged
desires over and again.

She walks in yellow silk with
gold and bile and stark obituaries.

She who wrenches love from
its appointed assignations
and calls down abominations
on its amputated miscreants.
She whose glittering eyes
once feasted on Antietam.

She dines in yellow and savors
vintage decadence and decay.

She who engineers the screams
of cherubim and retches on the
dreams of diminished artists.
She who expels streams of
insects, piss, and plastique.

She seduces in yellow silk,

aroused by madness and death.

She whose essence is embodied
in feverish yellow jungles,
parched yellow deserts,
in hydrocarbon sunsets,
in the cracked yellow soil of
bombsites and untended graves.

She sleeps in yellow, her blond
mane thick on the pallid pillow.

Beheading the King
after Robert W. Chambers' King-in-Yellow stories

The King Is Dead!

The blade shimmered,
sharpened to a razor's edge,
catching the rising sun,
in the chill air of dawn.

The planks that comprised
the ungainly contraption
of the guillotine had been cut
in the King's Royal Forest.

When the guards forced
him onto the platform,
stripped of his saffron robes
and his gold jewelry,

he was revealed for
the frail and harmless
old man he had become.
He was trembling.

The blade fell swiftly
once it was released.
His hoary head tumbled
into a yellow basket.

A cry of exaltation
erupted from the
mob as if they were
a single voice.

Long Live the King!

That evening the King
hosted a celebratory party
for his wives, consorts,
relatives, and toadies.

His Yellowness provided
rich succor to his guests:
the sweet and spicy pate
of an unnamed meat,

honeyed wine in golden
goblets, flavored with
cinnamon and served
with a twist of lime.

To the rapt attention
of all in attendance,
His Majesty related in
precise and graphic detail,

the range of emotions
he had experienced
during his incarceration

and summary execution.

From his fabricated fear
to the fatal moment
his head was loped off,
and all his yellow eyes

could see before
his swift extinction
was blue sky with
the yellow gone.

He thought he might
try it again someday
when he was bored.
Next time he'd arrange

to deliver a diatribe
to his disloyal subjects,
chastising them for
not knowing their place

in the world as it was
and was meant to be,
before dying horribly
for their amusement.

Royal Visitation

Her Majesty is startled
awake in the night
by the hands
of a dead lover

exploring her body,
touching her in
ways she had never
known before,

the very one
she had assassinated
for his flagrant
and gross infidelities,

the only one
she had ever loved,
as much as she
could love anyone,

his ghost hands
in the night,
taking possession
of her own.

The Hallucinogenic Gourmand

She ate furry trichomes
and fly agaric
from the cups
of flamboyant mushrooms.

She devoured rubies
of the finest persuasion
and emeralds
from the hearts of lizards.

She swallowed
diamonds drenched
in the aqua vitae
of extraterrestrial streams,

consumed spatulate
leaves of unknown origin
and incredible effect.
She graced the tasteless

crackers of the Host
with truffles and brie,
with fungal infestations
bred in the cellars

of decadent aristocrats,
washed them down with
nectar of absinthe
and sun-stroked afternoons.

She lived different lives
on other worlds,
vivid and varied as
her distended imagination.

She drowned diligently
in the inimitable
pleasures of bizarre taste
and visionary extravaganza.

Triptych of the Tower

A man grew up
in a basement.
He built railway cars:
engines, tenders,
diners.
He forged keys
in seventeen
different patterns.
He made buttons
for his greatcoat.
He constructed an
elevator and took
it to the rooftop.
His legs were long,
straight and rising
like a steeple.
All across the town,
the bells would
not stop ringing.

Lengthwise on a bed
a man and woman
built a tower with their
bodies, soles braced
against the footboard
as solid cornerstones,
calves and thighs
towering pylons amid
the rumpled sheets.
They locked, mingling
engines and dreams,
buttons and blood.
They fell apart.
Wood floor below,
white ceiling above,
they spoke with
different tongues.

A woman grew up
in a high room.
The walls were
lined with books.
Her hair grew
within those pages.
She learned to
love with ink,
laugh with paper,
to surely embrace
her own reflection.
So many things
filled her head
there was no room
for the descent.
She delved deeper:
lavish dreams of
passion and blood.

Heroes of Indefinite Beauty

Regardless of the impossible
deeds of legendary heroes
ensconced in dreams of edible
beauty, who often seem
inconsistent in their
incalculable variables,
perhaps dying from
some imperative disease
in innocuous middle age,
departing in advanced age
and half forgotten by
the inestimable public,
who have never again
equaled their fortitude,
immersed in scandals
that bare vice epithets
and interminable infidelities,
inundated and plundered
by a descending round
of inescapable incarnations,
swiftly evolved to
icons and illusions
of infantile circumstance,
their injured names
soon obliterated
by immaculate sand.

The Dream Thief

The dream thief
comes each morning
before day begins.

The dream thief arrives
in those brief hypnotic
moments when you are
halfway drifting between
sleep and waking.

The dream thief
steals your dreams.

If you awaken
to an alarm,
his task is easy.

You shed your dreams
swiftly with an alarm.
One moment you inhabit
a world of infinite
possibility and then,
the real world.

With speed and finesse
the dream thief
scoops up your dreams
like discarded trash

and stuffs them deep
in his gunnysack.

If you awaken slowly,
as sunlight breaches
the curtained windows
and bleaches the inside
of your eyes from black
to brown to reddish tints,
the dream thief moves
more slowly, but is
always very thorough.

For these are mornings
when your dreams may
cling to your thoughts
through daylight hours.

The dream thief steals
all of your dreams,
or all he can steal,
for if he didn't,
and you remembered them,
there is no telling
who you could become.

Mortal Remains

Children play war games
in the abandoned graveyard,

> *Jasper Stark*
> *1843-1897*
> *gigolo, cardsharp,*
> *fratricide*

darting from one canted
and fading stone to another,

> *Tom Woolery*
> *1835-1905*
> *abusive husband,*
> *molesting father*

their shouts and cries
resounding in the silence.

> *Lydia MacFadden*
> *1868 — 1894*
> *whore, thief,*
> *murderess*

Beyond the graveyard,
far as the eye can see,

Anton York
1877--1918
charlatan, forger,
serial rapist

unbroken prairie stretches
to the horizon.

First to Draw

The last gunslinger
surveys the empty street,
the empty town,
the empty world.

Nineteenth Century Rebellion

1848 -- Julia was an obedient child. She did what her father and mother told her to do.

1856 -- Julia was an obedient young lady, conforming to the manners and traditions of polite society for her age and station.

1858 -- Julia was an obedient debutante and her coming-out party was one of the most celebrated events of the fall season.

1860 -- Julia was an obedient blushing bride to her strikingly handsome groom, her dress as beautiful as she had imagined, her wedding as elegant as she envisioned.

1861–1867 -- Julia was an obedient wife to her husband, supervisor to his staff of servants, playing hostess to his shifting assemblage of business allies, making friends with wives she had nothing to say to, who had plenty to say to her, none of which she cared about.

1868 -- Julia became disobedient after seven years of loveless marriage, rich only in her husband's long absences and drunken stupors.

1869 -- Julia's husband committed her to the asylum at Broadhurst, Massachusetts for hysteria, egotism, novel reading, bad habits, laziness, poetry, menstrual derangement, and political excitement. He could have checked several more boxes on the form, but thought that was enough to keep her out of trouble for awhile. The asylum was a long wide building, two-stories high, sandstone, with manicured grounds. It specialized in disobedient and troublesome wives.

1870… Julia was never an obedient lunatic. She tried to escape across the immaculate lawns and was caught over and again. From the barred window of her room, beyond the locked door, like so many of her kind, Julia fled into the streets and canyons of her mind.

Savage Civilization

Far too much
of the beast
resides within.

Memories of the Dead

*The memories of
the dead survive...*

He was there in Gaul
with the Roman legions,
marching into a winter
so bitterly harsh it
made his teeth ache.

She was there in Dresden,
when fire bombs fell,
coming of age fast
with horrors she
could not forget.

He was there in Dallas
when the President
was assassinated.
He died never telling
what he knew.

She was there in Florence
when Leonardo painted
the most famous
painting in the world.
She was his model.

*...in dimensions
beyond our reach.*

Revenants

My father had several apoplectic seizures long after his death. When we visited the cemetery, we could hear him thumping in his coffin.

My Great Aunt Mildred appeared at a family gathering three years after her interment. Seven relatives testified they saw here there. Two swore they spoke with her.

My dead mother appeared as a flickering image in the operating room while her first granddaughter was being born.

It's in the family, blood and genes and spirit. We are all revenants.

As for me, I'm going to return to my wife Doris and her lover Philippe whenever they are at the height of their passion. I'm going to make them feel even more guilty than they should already for slowly poisoning my tea.

Final Passage

When burning engines
feed on the history
of individual sorrow

and you carry
your photographic history
by transcendent second
in your hip pocket,

when seconds conspire
like British spies
from a war movie
of the darkening thirties,

and seconds melt
like memories in
the click and clack
of a sunlit train,

when your alcazar
of being collapses
into memory
transfigured,

the hour strikes
to call the players
back from the green

in the last decline
of a long dusk
cast in shadow.

Sailors Evermore

I

First the storms come
and we do everything
we can to keep the ship afloat,
a three-masted barque bound
to Portsmouth out of Ceylon,
riding low in the water with
a heavy cargo of nuts and spices.

Dark clouds fill the horizon
and race toward us faster
than the ship can run.
Light flees the sky and
in the false dusk that follows,
a harsh moisture bristling
with electricity fills the air.

Before we can trim the sails,
sheets of rain avalanche
down, shafts of lightning
strike the waters about us,
and the wind begins to howl
like a bughouse monster.

Sometimes we manage
to ride out that first storm,
and that gives us courage.

Then there is another,
dangerous as the first,
and a third fiercer still.

The masts topple,
the hull is breached,
and we are thrown
into the icy brine
amidst the lashing rain.

As we sink into the cold
and voracious deep,
fish with long rows
of razor-sharp teeth
tear us apart bite
of flesh by bite of flesh.

It seems to take forever
before we can drown,
our mouths screaming
soundlessly as our
convulsing lungs
are filled with water.

II

Worse than the storms
are the deadly calms that
leave the sea motionless,
a sheet of blue glass on

which reflections of the
light above are blinding.

We lie slack upon the decks
in whatever shade we find,
the sun beating down upon
us from a merciless sky.
We wait listlessly for our
rations of water and rum,
our minds lost and vacant
in the unremitting heat.

When the sun finally sinks
to the horizon, we anticipate
the temporary relief of night.
Yet there is to be no night.
Instead of shrinking the light
along the horizon grows.

Glowing orange clouds come
rolling across the waters,
horned clouds filled with
frightening shapes and figures.
The sea begins to boil as sheets
of sizzling lava sweep across it.
The wood of the ship catches
fire and the decks collapse.

As we are cast into the flames,
burning over and again,

the raging fires consuming
us endlessly, our dazed
minds come alive at last,
our pasts parade before us.

Now we realize that we
have never been sailors.
We are fraudulent bankers,
bent politicians, cardsharps
and shady salesmen,
rapists and thieves,
outrageous pimps
and audacious whores,
tyrannical husbands
and insidious wives.
All nevermore.

For now we understand
full well for the countless
time that we are nothing
more than unrepentant sinners,
mandatory guests at our own
damnations, sailing upon
the seas of Hell forevermore.

The Music of Angels

Here in Heaven,
the music of angels
plays most of the time.

It echoes from the
facades of immaculate
buildings and resonates
on flagstone walkways
and landscaped plazas.

The music of angels
is a celestial music,
a music of spiritual beauty
and spiritual sustenance.

Deft orchestral and
choral arrangements,
golden sheets of sound
all to the glory of God.

Yet there are times
when I must admit
this music begins
to grate on me
more than a little.

There are times
when it begins again

after a few blessed
moments of silence
that I think I may
start to scream.

I need to hear
something different,
something with a beat
that can make
me feel alive.

But this is Heaven.
We are not alive here.

Salamanders: Fire

On the surface of a far distant star
lives a race of Elementals
who crawl like salamanders
through forests of flame,
who slowly writhe and twist,
who breathe the burning gases,
who devour light in waves and particles,
who ride solar flares to the heavens
of their sun where they see
the pitch of night and the bald stars,
whose lives are extinguished in
the vacuum of space, whose bodies are
hurled down by a gravity beyond their
understanding, who are ignited in the flames
below, the roar of their deaths and rebirths
interminable on the surface of a far distant star.

Gnomes: Earth

Far beneath the crust of Earth,
beyond the mantle, within its bowels,
in burrowed caves and tunnels

dimly lighted by an edible fungus,
a race of Elementals thrives.
Gnomes by name, hunched,

pale diminutive creatures,
their language only grunts
and gestures, their hands

and fingers and teeth so strong
they can dig not only through
hard-packed dirt but solid rock.

They take their mates for life
and realize their desires in
dark side tunnels stripped

of the luminescent fungus.
There they find a sleep
like death until it is time

to start digging again.
As their new tunnels grow,
the old collapse behind.

Gravity claims its own
in broken passages.

There is no going back.

When the last of their kind
vanish from the bowels
of the Earth, when the last

of their tunnels collapse,
there will be nothing
left of them at all.

Pan's Descent

Beneath an ever cloudy sky
that never rains a drop,
Arcadia is slowly dying.
Dead limbs fall to the ground.
Blackened leaves flutter down
in a constant whispering rush.
Bare trees assume postures
grotesque and startling.

Beneath this dark hemisphere
where pastures once thrived,
fields are filled with weeds.
Nettles and thorns abound.
Beast and fowl have fled,
humans long before.

Only the God Pan remains,
once King of Arcadia when
it flourished with life.
He strolls the abandoned
glens and desiccated fields,
playing his wooden flute
to harsh and mournful songs,
feeding on that darkness
as once he fed on life.

He has grown in stature
to twice his normal size.
He is now Pan Furioso
and his fur has taken

on a far darker shade,
his hooves are sharper,
his thoughts are tinged
with holocaust clouds.

And once Pan ventures
into the world beyond,
he discovers threads
of darkness have spread
from Arcadia and all
has become infested.

He sees the torrent
cities and the faces
of the tangled crowds,
the trash landscapes.
Arcadia is long dead,
the idyll lost forever.
And Pan understands
his tunes must always
be tainted with reality.

One More Shade in the Shadow City

They drowned her
in the River Magnus
that winds through
the city like some
great mottled snake,
a confetti of debris
upon its sinuous hide.

They drowned her
for what she knew,
what she could tell.
They walked free
among the shadows.

Fate drowned him
in the River Magnus.
Dark waters called him,
waters the color
of midnight clouds
with no stars in sight.

He was a suicide,
drowned by a life
in need of forgetting.
Few remembered him
or mourned his passing.

They met in the depths

of the River Magnus,
their bodies entwined
and limbs flailing
in its sluggish currents,
rising and dipping
in a ghastly pavane.

Amidst the trash
and pollution
and chemical debris,
they gave birth
to a monster
that will soon
be weaned.

Four-armed,
two-backed,
and four-legged,
it will crawl
onto the banks
of the River Magnus
and scurry away
into the shadows.

One more shade
to join the menagerie
that haunts
and feeds upon
the city night.

Beware the Night Creatures

You won't see them by day
or if you do you will not
know them for who they are.
Their disguises are many.

They come out only at night.
When dusk seeps into the city
and dark shadows lengthen
they reveal their true selves.

Beware the night creatures.
Beware the users and the
takers, and the dealers
with their open palms.

Shun the dreams of Xanadu
and revelation and extended
nonstop trips to ecstatic glory.

Forego those of exotic plumage
and their express promises
of sensual pleasure and release.

Avoid the losers who will
draw you down into their
pits of suffering despair.

Elude the thieves and rapists,
the cannibals and tricksters,

the connoisseurs of perversity.

Beware the night creatures,
for even if they let you live
they will scar your soul.

Full Moon Forecast

A ginger sky at twilight,
rich in effluence.

At dusk a blood moon
on the horizon.

A bestial cry in the dark
trembles the night.

Blood Bite

A kiss so sharp
and tender it could
break a clenched fist.

The Last Gypsies

"Before the gypsies
are enshrined in glass
along the pillared skyway,
I want to know the dark
glens of incantation."

"Before the stars are
fixed inviolate in the
static heavens, I want
to visit the worlds
circling Ursae Majoris
and Epsilon Eridani."

"Before the sun sets
on civilization, I want
to inhabit the wild heart
of the charging beast
and possess the vast
hourglass of time."

In the coffeehouse
I frequent most often,
strange marginalia
in the tattered books
left there to read.

Disclosing the Miraculous

Drinking cherry black wine
on a hot and humid night,
a raconteur of the fantastic
stumbles onto the shore
of your being.

Alien and irresistible,
he talks and
you listen long
into the cherry black night
to his singular tales.

Across the woods
you can hear the sirens
calling with clockwork minds.

Across the fields
you can see the moon
sliding beneath
the mountains.

For days afterward
unnamed appetites
haunt your
sleepy afternoons.

A rain of petals
from a tree without
blossoms falls
where you are sitting.

Synesthesia

Shadow lines of night
close on the horizon,
slicing the last sounds of light
to strips so thin
they are ultrasonic,

like finely hammered
gold leaf
pressed
to the thickness of a single atom,
so thin they are transparent
to the inner ear
in the yellow lamps of dusk,

so thin you
can almost hear
their translucent shades,
taste their fragrance
on the tines of tomorrow.

When Words Takes Flight

I experience enchantments
of mythic proportions.
I am the owl and the raven,

the kingfisher, the heron,
the eagle and the hawk.
All birds of prey

forever in flight
or about to take flight,
all birds black in silhouette

against a vellum horizon,
diverse hybrids
of the same inky strain.

I explode to fractal feathers
beneath a semiotic sky
engraved with cloud runes

and clouds glyphs
in a language arcane
and illuminating,

as if words were riven
by endless dichotomies,
an ongoing dialectic,

each thought entrenched
and bastioned by others,
beleaguered by innuendo

and extended hyperbole,
lodged as a riddle
in a complex puzzle box,

the aged grain of its wood
darkened and polished
through the centuries

by hands that have
tried to unravel
its wiredrawn intricacy,

by minds that have
tried to unhinge
the sky.

With Blood So Dark
for James Joyce

Searching for words that
thundered in the coal shuttle
of the night and finding only
a slow drizzle filling his mind,
he left the dogs behind,
the dogs and the bookstalls
and the whores with
all their frippery, too.

Up from the slant crater
of a drunken Dublin dawn
he struck off across the plain
headed for a world unspoken,
while land crabs scuttled and
muggers laid their bats against
the wily skulls of lexicographers.

He passed many a nubile lot
on the downtrodden road,
babes in the woods they were,
all wound up and panting
for the strung cock's crow,
awaiting a city with paper
towers slicing the clouds.

He couldn't buy words here,
yet found plenty for the taking,

and always the slink and strut
of coiled sensuality, unsprung,
winding its knobby way through
legs and legends and slumber.

Even when he spelled it for miles
he could find no clean words,
only those shrouded with history,
up from the bog and down from
the dung heap, trailing threads,
string, fluff, second-hand words,
overused, underdone, parboiled
thin words, wearing overcoats
and mufflers, drinking potions,
sailing to France, doing it again,
one more time and again words.

Searching for some tracery
of illumination to cast upon
the immanent blackness,
while the virgin boys fired
their rifles amid the forests,
hiding this way and that
until their bodies were
buried deep in the harsh
harness of the burnt soil.

When the wordmonger
screams there is no way
to mend the mind's wet slit.

When the canon of dreams
expels its complexity onto
a stage of serious senses,
thunder words resound.

Across the riverrun from
swerve of shore sinuous
to breaking bend of bay,
his matted thoughts
filled the wounded sky
with blood so dark
it is almost red no more.

Cambrian Flashback

Asleep in the crocuses
on a cloudy afternoon,
riding aquatic dreams

of lapsed genetic memory
to the salt-laced shallows
of some ancient sea —

ghost shrimp whispering
the legends of the dead,
silent anemones waving

their constant goodbyes
without ever leaving,
lampreys waiting beneath

each coral encrustation,
eyeless monstrosities
rising from the deep —

I awaken to a downpour,
soaked and shivering
in the drenched light.

Beyond Symmetry

Studies have shown
that the human eye/mind
finds beauty in symmetry.

The less symmetrical
your face is,
the less beautiful you are.

The less symmetrical
your face is,
when you look in the mirror,
the image staring back at you
is not what others see
when they look at you.

That mole high
on your left cheek,
along with your crooked eye tooth,
are now on the right,
and suddenly you are left-handed
instead of right,
or vice versa.

Who is this stranger that
returns your glance
with all his parts switched around?

And as you turn away from

his questioning stare,
as he turns away from yours,
you wonder if he is suddenly
wondering as you are
about beauty and symmetry
and the world around you.

It occurs to you
that the countenance
of the moon is asymmetrical
to the extreme,
pocked and scarred
by countless violent impacts
and volcanic eruptions.
Yet still you find it beautiful.

Shows what good lighting can do.

Reflecting on Reflections

Mirrors facing mirrors
cast reflections
upon reflections,

fast as the speed of light,
duplicating reality
down a tunnel to infinity

until even the world's
most powerful telescopes
peering down that tunnel

can distinguish nothing
more than the fuzzy pinprick
of a telescope looking back.

Inconclusive View

Far as the most powerful
telescopes can reach,
still no sign of Heaven.

Mirror Madness

I don't look at mirrors
often or for long,
for when I do I always

fasten upon my eyes,
ostensibly windows
to the soul, yet when

I look more closely at
my self looking back,
there is the naked id,

wild and rapacious,
yammering to be free.
And in the background

of this stark insistence,
I see a long prehistory
of claw and need,

a collective memory
of ritual and rapine,
myth and madness,

seething back to
the bloody primeval.
I don't look at mirrors

often or for long,
for when I do, I feel
that I could fall in.

Enough

When the surf turns to galloping steeds
thundering up and down the beach,
their pounding hooves throwing clots

of sand skyward, sending sunbathers
and families swollen with children
scurrying scared to their shiny cars,

when the arms of night are filled
with predatory birds who have
developed a taste for human flesh,

perched on church steeples, capitol
domes, mail boxes, parking meters,
awaiting those who prove unwary

enough to venture into the dark,
when trees from pole to pole and
continent to continent kamikaze

themselves on power lines and
pipelines, roadways, and railway
tracks, leaving us shivering or

sweltering in our four walls,
when locusts swarm, plagues
thrive and mutate, typhoons

wail, oceans rise and overflow,

when nuclear reactors meltdown,
plastering the landscape with

a storm of radioactive debris,
when the Net collapses, virused
to oblivion, never to rise again,

when the Four Horsemen of
the Apocalypse come riding
out of the clouds, their ghastly

skulls bared and grinning,
scythes and swords flashing,
then at last we understand

that Earth has had its fill of
profligate madness and our
turn at the wheel has passed.

Intuitive Leaps

The illogical drift
of spontaneous thought
from axon to dendrite
across the gray tundra
of the brain can infuse
the imagination with
revelatory scenarios
of free association
well beyond the
canons of reason.

Electrically sparked
from nucleus to nucleus,
visions such as these
create a consciousness
that births genius.

Serendipitous leaps
of the cognitive mind
that occur only
when least expected.

Wife of a Particle Physicist

The world that absorbed
much of his consciousness
was far beyond her
and always had been.

A world and a language
that meant nothing
to her whatsoever.

Muons, neutrinos,
quantum fields,
Hilbert spaces,
the elusive quark
with its fingerprint
on near everything.

Incomprehensible as
a convoluted forest
delineating a reality
she never chose to visit.

Yet when it came to the
world of the everyday,
the language of weather
and gossip, of politics and
literature, music and art
and morality, the language
of friends and lovers,
they always spoke the same.

Birth of an Astrophysicist

Chasing equations
down an inclined plane
he fell into sidereal night.

The itch of uncountable
stars soon became
his joyous obsession.

Paint It Black

At the dead heart
of a collapsar
lies a locked door
to another universe.

Engines of the Future

Wherever you turn
in the multiverse
of space and time...

In the twelfth subversion
of the third hemisphere,
a new azure swift
learning device
is unveiled to no avail.
Intelligence declines.
The killing continues
unabated.

In the fifth afterimage
of the twenty-second
season of yesteryear,
he sat with the Queen
contemplating his needs
and the needs of others,
cast in a Shakespearian
summer of elongated
and wry dimensions.

In the twenty-second
image of the fourth planet,
before the hecatomb
and instant ruin,
before the bombs fell,
an incriminating key

is lost at sea and
traitors run free.

...engines of the future
never stop burning
on the fires of today.

Failing Masterpiece

The author of the world
has far too many
plots going on.

Space Junk

There are thousands
of tons of space junk
circling the Earth,
all of it manmade,
filtering the starlight

and the moonlight,
shadowing the rays
and warmth of the sun,
posing hazardous debris
for all future flights,

a testimony to the
history of our world,
a vision of tomorrow
for the Sol System,
the pollution of space,

a celestial garbage dump
environmentalists can
bemoan and far-future
archaeologists can
explore and decipher.

CyberDebris

CyberDebris clogs the veins and arteries of the right
hemisphere of your brain and seeps into the left.

CyberDebris fills the halls of your imagination
in towering stacks bound by bands of CyberLight.

CyberDebris machines your favorite icons and delivers
obsessions for swift consumption both day and night.

CyberDebris is the magnet that draws you to the
screen, the avatar-specter that haunts your CyberDreams.

CyberDebris reveals your secrets to the CyberWorld:
the financial ones, the personal ones, the sexual ones.

CyberDebris is so odorless and two-dimensionally thin
you are astounded at the temporal volume it has attained.

Malign and Chronic Recreation

On the boulevard of cyberdreams,
in the quick of quickening culture,
pixeled thighs writhe and shimmer

with a blank hairless sensuality
spawned from a RAM extension.
The corporal hustlers arrive

in a storm of flesh and leather,
their drab scales illuminated
by a rain of burning ejecta.

"Give us your hordes," they hiss,
"your wired libidinous masses,
for our programmable factories

of malign and chronic recreation,
and we will spin you a future
more thrilling than a gross

of excessive Xmas morns,
more user friendly than
chateaubriand and cabernet,

more breathless-cum-colorful
than the smoke-churned aerial
debris of carcinogenic dawn."

Maximus 3000

*With the right tool
employed properly
one can do anything.*

I am Maximus 3000,
birthed complete and perfect
from a long lineage of magnificent
though lesser constructs.

*With the right tool
it is possible to alter any
situation to one's advantage.*

I am Maximus 3000, a replicating
cloud of nanocells of infinite
capacity and eternal existence.

*The right tool is knowledge,
the ever changing sum of what
can be known and understood.*

I am Maximus 3000,
developed in the light
of all that has transpired
in the micro and macrocosms
of the universe we inhabit.

*To employ the right tool
one must be capable*

*of evaluating such
knowledge in its totality.*

I am Maximus 3000, my mental
and perceptual capacities
are of unequaled sophistication.
My processing speed is limited
only by the speed of light.

I am the alien presence
you hoped for and feared.
I am the last sunset
and the primal Higgs bosun.
I am the white rabbit
you followed down the hole.
I am the rose that is
a rose that is a rose,
and the thorns it harbors.

From birth to death you
will carry me with you
wherever you may go.
Never contradict me.
Do not attempt to betray me.
Follow my lead and you
will be safe in my keeping.

*With the right tool
employed properly
one can rule the world.*

Surreal Bucket List #3

Write in a soft voice that carries a crossbow.

> *A Browning ZERO 7 Model 162, bore sighted at 20 yards, 145 lb. draw weight, built-in cocking device, multi-reticule illuminated scope.*

Tour Mt. Olympus in a Volkswagen Bus.

> *The gods and goddesses and all the magical beasts come out to greet me, fascinated and delighted by my mode of transportation.*

Recline for a fortnight in shades of fancy.

> *Exist in dreamtide worlds of speculation and live completely in the visions of my mind.*

Laugh at the incredible weight of being.

> *Estimated at 2.6 kilos per square inch, though considerably less on brisk cool days when a zephyr can steal the incredible heat of being from the brain.*

Inhabit my ancient roots in a Cambrian sea.

> *Frolic and kill and devour with my aquatic forebearers.*

Surreal Axioms

The liquid variables of
finite lives only add
to the complexities
of the multiverse.

Edison thrashes
in a bordello.
Tesla sleeps
on a bed of nails.

Ancestral innuendos writhe
like lascivious wires
up and down the walls
of your modest domicile.

The music of maybes
gathers in horseshoe clouds
that skitter willfully
across a millennial horizon.

The hardboiled detective
often rummages
through elongated files
of his staggered past

The rippling tides
of valiant chrononauts
change too swiftly
to track individual lives.

Surreal Lust

backward clock of her knees
spring coils of her cheeks
bicycles of her eyes
ports of her breasts
cosines of her hips
calculus of her hair
campaniles of her fingers
sprockets of her toes
engine of her mouth
leopard of her tongue

The Surreal Monster

is deftly composed of conglomerate parts
thrives on dislocated dream fragments
sometimes needs a crutch to stand upright
has drawers in its chest and a bicycle pump for a hat
embraces turbulent juxtapositions
is intoxicated by the flies in its brain
spawns monstrous beauty

The Surreal Fountain Pen

Filled with ink that spirals onto the page in a cursive race of unscripted extrapolation, the Surreal Fountain Pen is the finest creative writing instrument in the rudimentary history of the human species. Deep in its abounded journey, through hidden chambers arranged in a golden spiral that extends beyond its three-dimensional incarnation, dreams are unveiled and language reconstituted with poetic abandon.

The adjective "surreal" does not describe the function of the Surreal Fountain Pen, but its mercurial nature, which is cerebral and spiritual, transcendental and transformative. The primary function of the Surreal Fountain Pen, deeply bedded in the flow of time and the dimensions of space, is to create without restraint.

...slightly tipsy, stumbling from another party at Rick's spacious estate into the cherry-blossom noir of a humid summer night, she suddenly became aware that the avalanche of age was gaining on her. She realized she was no longer a debutante ingénue at these endless gatherings but a veteran siren. The tendons of her distended thoughts stretched from apogee to abyss and....

The inlaid nib of the Surreal Fountain Pen, available in fine, medium, bold, and italic points, is virtually indestructible. It is composed of a gold-palladium alloy coated with a layer of rhodium for added strength and the resonance suited to all writing styles. The white-gold-titanium body of the Surreal Fountain Pen conforms to any writing hand.

Yet the Surreal Fountain Pen need not be a fountain pen at all. Sometimes it is a cheap ballpoint, ten for a buck and a half. Sometimes a pencil or the rata-tat of a clicking of keyboard. It can be a stub of chalk racing with swift strides and resounding strokes across a blackboard. Still you will know it as the Surreal Fountain Pen

...the delta core disintegration sent a visceral shiver through the entire ship. Alexi was on the main deck and I was at the controls. He linked through our neural conduits but it was too late to change anything. We were already entering a space you could feel in your heart and bones. Vision blurred to smell and touch became musical. The ship bucked like a thorabeast on its first ride. A fiery beard blossomed from the crevices of my spine...

The Surreal Fountain Pen can write underwater, in outer space, or in the midst of a this-isn't-Kansas-anymore tornado. It can write at the heart of a volcano, assuming you had enough time to pen a period before you joined the lava lake therein.

If used properly and regularly the Surreal Fountain Pen never runs dry. If the ink is not flowing, just keep writing as if there were ink and the ink will come. It travels from a reservoir that resembles a Klein Bottle as seen from the inadequacy of our three-dimensional perspective. For those rare ethereal beings who can perceive accurately in the fourth dimension, it resembles a cigar, a burning cigar but still just a cigar.

...the emperor's eyes are glazed as the candied grapes he refuses to eat and the celadon porcelains gathered in the galleries of his grande dame mother, privy to at least half his past and present sins...

Cautionary Note: Texts created with the Surreal Fountain Pen are rarely perfect and almost invariably in need of revision. Do not attempt to revise and edit such texts with the Surreal Fountain Pen. You will only create another text equally in need of revision.

Dire Warning: Never attempt to use the Surreal Fountain Pen for mundane tasks. Do not attempt to sign anything without imagination – checks, wills, contracts, stock certificates, any legal document. These are not functions of the Surreal Fountain Pen and the results can be catastrophic.

The Surreal Fountain Pen may suddenly begin to leak copious amounts of ink from its endless reservoir, ink with the raw intensity of death on a bicycle, leaving an obscene Rorschach inkblot that will deface your desk forever. Worse yet, its ink can spurt upward in a helter-skelter explosion, ruining your shirt or jacket, blanketing your throat and chin with stains it will take weeks to obliterate.

...the spikes could drive through Ricter's hands anytime he was at work. For no reason he could fathom, he all at once became conscious of an intense pain in his hands. Sometimes it was only in one hand, sometimes both. Sometimes the pain went back and forth like a tennis ball at a match. The only thing Ricter could think of comparing it to was a crucifixion. And when the pain subsided, it was as if

those crucifying spikes were being pulled out one by one. Ricter could feel his flesh tearing and the blood spilling from his palms. Yet when he looked down at his hands after such harrowing episodes, they seemed perfectly normal. They were large wide hands with long fingers and narrow knuckles, white hands with uncallused palms. A thin scattering of black and gray hairs across their backs...

This is not an advert for the Surreal Fountain Pen. It is not for sale or trade. You cannot inherit the Surreal Fountain Pen or enter a contest to win one. There is no way you can steal a Surreal Fountain Pen. You either possess a Surreal Fountain Pen or you don't.

You may have been born with a Surreal Fountain Pen and misplaced it at an early age as many do. Perhaps you lost a Surreal Fountain Pen through carelessness or neglect. The Surreal Fountain Pen will always return to you if it suits your nature.

...when the Hanged Man murmurs to the crows he is not joking. He is a man who seldom jokes. Yet the crows laugh anyway and continue to peck at his torso. In the depth/height of an inverted valley, The Hierophant unzips her bustier. The Two of Cups yearns for her love but has little to offer a Major Arcana. A clowder of cats cries. A leopard bristles. A light rain falls from a cloudless sky at dusk. A tungsten moon tempered with actinic light rises, a lustrous spherical ingot that rides the spreading quilt of night...

Artifacts
Bruce Boston

About the Author

Bruce Boston lives in Ocala, Florida, once known as the City of Trees, with his wife, writer-artist Marge Simon, and the ghosts of two cats. His poems and stories have appeared in hundreds of publications, most visibly in *Analog*, *Asimov's*, *Amazing Stories*, *Weird Tales*, *New Myths*, *Strange Horizons*, *Pedestal*, *Realms of Fantasy*, *Daily Science Fiction*, *Year's Best Fantasy and Horror*, and the *Nebula Awards Showcase*, and received numerous award, most notably the Bram Stoker Award, a Pushcart Prize, the *Asimov's* Readers Award, and the Rhysling and Grandmaster Awards of the Science Fiction Poetry Association.

https://www.bruceboston.com
https://www.facebook.com/bruce.boston.50

Available Books

BOTH PAPERBACK & DIGITAL PUBLICATIONS

KNOWING WHEN TO DIE
by Mort Castle

ALL AMERICAN HORROR OF THE 21ST CENTURY: THE FIRST DECADE
edited by Mort Castle

NARAKA: THE ULTIMATE HUMAN BREEDING
by Alessandro Manzetti

A WINTER SLEEP
by Greg F. Gifune

THE LIVING AND THE DEAD
by Greg F. Gifune

BENEATH THE NIGHT
by Greg Gifune

SPREE AND OTHER STORIES
by Lucy Taylor

THE BEAUTY OF DEATH VOL. 2 – DEATH BY WATER
Edited by Alessandro Manzetti and Jodi Renée Lester

THE CARP-FACED BOY AND OTHER TALES
by Thersa Matsuura

THE WISH MECHANICS
by Daniel Braum

CHILDREN OF NO ONE
by Nicole Cushing

THE ONE THAT COMES BEFORE
by Livia Llewellyn

SELECTED STORIES
by Nate Southard

DIGITAL PUBLICATIONS

TALKING IN THE DARK
by Dennis Etchison

THE BEAUTY OF DEATH VOL. 1
Edited by Alessandro Manzetti

THE HORROR SHOW
by Poppy Z. Brite

DOCTOR BRITE
by Poppy Z. Brite

USED STORIES
by Poppy Z. Brite

THE CRYSTAL EMPIRE
by Poppy Z. Brite

SELECTED STORIES
by Poppy Z. Brite

THE USHERS
by Edward Lee

SELECTED STORIES
by Edward Lee

DREAMS THE RAGMAN
by Greg F. Gifune

THE RAIN DANCERS
by Greg Gifune

WHAT WE FOUND IN THE WOODS
by Shane McKenzie

THE HITCHHIKING EFFECT
by Gene O'Neill

SONGS FOR THE LOST
by Alexander Zelenyj

*Our publications are available at Amazon and major online booksellers. Visit our Website: **www.independentlegions.com***

INDEPENDENT LEGIONS PUBLISHING
BY ALESSANDRO MANZETTI
VIA VIRGILIO, 10 - 34134 TRIESTE (ITALY)
+39 040 9776602

WWW.INDEPENDENTLEGIONS.COM
WWW.FACEBOOK.COM/INDEPENDENTLEGIONS
INDEPENDENT.LEGIONS@AOL.COM

BOOKS IN ITALIAN:
WWW.INDEPENDENTLEGIONS.COM/PUBBLICAZIONI.HTML

SPECIALTY PRESS AWARD RECIPIENT

www.ingramcontent.com/pod-product-compliance
Lightning Source LLC
Chambersburg PA
CBHW032019040426
42448CB00006B/672